THE GREAT CONFESSION

by

Larry D. Rudder

Faith and Family Focus Series

RudderHaven

3014 Washington Ave

Granite City, IL 62040

Published by:
RudderHaven
3014 Washington Ave
Granite City, IL 62040
USA

First Softcover Printing, July 2016, RudderHaven
(978-1-932060-18-8)

Cover Design: Sheri L. Rudder

Neither the artist, the author, nor the publisher make any claim to any and all third-party 3D models, textures, or other materials used in the creation of the cover art. All copyrights for third-party materials belong to the individual creators and/or producers of those materials. Used under license. The artist only claims the copyright of the finished derivative art.

Printed in the United States of America

ISBN 978-1-932060-18-8

A Special Thanks. . . .

To the editors and publishers in my family who spent many hours preparing the manuscript for publication.

To my wife, Jeanette Rudder (M.A.) for editing and proofing the complete manuscript.

To my son, Douglas, who prepared the manuscript for publication, including editing, layout, and design.

To my daughter-in-law, Sheri, who designed the cover art.

Contents

Meet for the Master's Use.................................1

He is Lord!..10

Are You Acceptable?.....................................16

A New and Living Way.................................26

Examine Yourself...43

The Lordship of Christ.................................53

.

Meet for the Master's Use:

*But in a great house there are not only
vessels of gold and of silver, but also of
wood and of earth; and some to honour,
and some to dishonour. If a man therefore purge himself from these, he shall
be a vessel unto honour, sanctified, and
meet for the Master's use, and prepared
unto every good work.* **[2 Timothy 2:20–21]**

When it comes to the personality and nature of our
Creator, people often fail to recognize Him for who He
really is, and what He means to every living creature on
Earth. Some people call Him "Mother Nature;" some
refer to Him as "the Man upstairs." Still others refuse
to recognize Him at all—perhaps hoping He will just
overlook them altogether.

God has made Himself known to man in the person
of His only begotten Son Jesus Christ. Christ is called
in Scripture the King of kings and Lord of lords. He is
also known under many other labels or personal charac-
teristics which we will discuss in this book. But where
you and I are concerned there is only one title that we
need to recognize in this life. He is the *Lord Jesus Christ*.
Each part of that name and title has a particular relevance
to your life—an essential element where your hope for
eternal life is concerned.

Christians tend to believe what they believe because
it's what they've been taught. I was actually confronted
by a fundamental minister once who declared that he
didn't care what the Bible said because his church held a

different view from the New Testament verses we were reading. On another occasion a young lady told me that she couldn't understand the Bible so she just had to accept what she was taught. I thought, *How sad! Why, my youngest son read and understood the Authorized Version of the Bible, J.R.R. Tolkien, and other such reading material when he was in grade school.* I'm afraid the young lady's view of the Bible was rooted in her unwillingness to "study to show herself approved unto God," or she was simply too lazy to read it for herself. And how many times I've heard people state their confidence in certain issues based on the fact that their pastors, or great preachers (and some not so great) in history have held those views. Some have trusted their knowledge of the Scriptures to the voices that pour from their radios and televisions. While some of those voices are true to the Word of God, many are not, and it isn't always easy to distinguish between the good and the bad. No one should ever surrender his or her reasoning and spiritual acumen to anyone else. In other words, you are solely responsible for your relationship with Christ and your depth of the knowledge His Word.

A correct understanding of God's Word requires a lot of prayer and a lot of work. The fact is that if we enter our studies with our minds made up about everything, we're not going to learn anything. We must *study* the Bible to discover truths that we might otherwise miss, and if we think we already know everything, then why study at all?

The fact is that we are all subject to our own abilities to reason things out. Sometimes we are right, and sometimes we are wrong. It's often because we don't spend the time in prayer and the study of God's Word, or listen to the still, small voice of the Holy Spirit who offers us the light of the Word, and we fail to turn the light on! I, for one, will never be satisfied with my knowledge of God's Word. After fifty-four plus years of Bible study and preaching, I'm constantly learning, and the more time and effort I put into my studies, the greater my understanding becomes—and the more surprises I find—especially when I discover that I was in the right ballpark but swinging at the wrong pitches. Yet, I will never reach the point when I am satisfied with what little I know. After all, John tells us that "there are also many other things which Jesus did, the which, if they should be written every one, I suppose that even the world could not contain the books that should be written" (John 21:25).

In 2 Timothy 2:15, Paul said, "Study to shew thyself approved unto God, a workman that needeth not to be ashamed, rightly dividing [literally: *dissecting*] the word of truth." If God's people fail to grasp the urgency in this verse, we will utterly fail the Lord.

If we discover something that seems to contradict what we have always believed, then we need to know why. Rather than simply accepting it or explaining it away, we need to work through it. So let's delve deeper into the Word to discover the importance of the Lordship of Christ in our lives.

Who is Jesus Christ? What does He mean to you? What is your relationship, if any, to Him? As my wife, Jeanette, and I have traveled from coast to coast preaching and singing the message of the hope of salvation, an issue has often arisen among many Christian fundamentalists regarding the Lordship of Jesus Christ resulting in a deep division among evangelicals. Sounds ludicrous, doesn't it? I find it unconscionable that anyone would choose to fight and divide the Church over such an issue—but it's just those types of things that have divided the Church for centuries. Let me make my position clear. If you are a born-again Christian, Jesus Christ is your Lord. If Jesus Christ is not your Lord, you are not a born-again Christian. Clear enough?

It's no wonder that the Church is experiencing a great "falling away" from the Lord of glory in these last days when men want to accept Christ as their Savior—but not confess Him as their Lord! That, of course, is a denial of His lordship. Since Paul tells us that we must confess Jesus as Lord in order to be saved in Romans 10:9, where he said "if thou shalt confess with thy mouth Jesus as Lord, and shalt believe in thine heart that God hath raised him from the dead, thou shalt be saved," committing our lives to Christ as our Lord is the beginning of our salvation experience. That commitment opens the door to Heaven and the throne of Almighty God. It is His lordship that authorizes His position as Savior.

The third chapter of John is probably cited more often among Christian believers than any other portion of Scripture. In fact, many unbelievers have memorized one particular verse—the focal point of that chapter, of all of John's Gospel, and perhaps of the entire Bible—John 3:16: "For God so loved the world, that he gave his only begotten Son, that whosoever believeth in him should not perish, but have everlasting life." But there are many more passages in John's Gospel that require our undivided attention.

The third chapter truly sheds light on the Lord Jesus Christ and our relationship with (or without) Him, and is perhaps the most often quoted section of the Bible used to lead unbelievers to faith in Him. It begins with the account of a man who walks in darkness but comes to the Light of life with the most important question a man could ask of God, but who never openly asks it. His name is Nicodemus, a Pharisee, a ruler of the Jews, and member of the court of seventy elders known as the Sanhedrin Council. "The same came to Jesus *by night*, and said unto him, Rabbi [*my Master*], we know that thou art a teacher come from God: for no man can do these miracles that thou doest, except God be with him" (John 3:2).

Nicodemus' recognition of who Jesus was went beyond the norm for a man of his position and power. In darkness, he called out to Him, "Rabbi [Greek, from the Hebrew, *Rhabbi*, meaning: *my Master*], we know that thou art a teacher come from God: for no man can do these miracles that thou doest, except God be with him."

First, note that Nicodemus called Jesus, "my Master." The term used was one of great honor. There is no place in the New Testament that refers to Jesus as being made a Jewish rabbi, but He was indeed recognized as *the* Master as He dealt with those who sought after Him. In verse 10, Jesus said of Nicodemus, "Art thou a master [Greek *didaskalos* meaning: *instructor* or *teacher*] of Israel, and knowest not these things?" So when Nicodemus said, "my Master," he was calling Jesus the *Master of teachers*." It was a unique statement expressing his confidence in who Jesus really was. At the same time, when Jesus called Nicodemus a master, He clarified the subordinate position that the man held—subordinate to the Master of teachers.

Jesus is the only person in the Bible who is called by this title except John the Baptist, who on one occasion

5

was inappropriately called Rabbi by his own disciples when they asked him about Jesus in John 3:26, "And they came unto John, and said unto him, Rabbi, he that was with thee beyond Jordan, to whom thou bearest witness, behold, the same baptizeth, and all men come to him."

In Matthew 23:6–10, Jesus warns the disciples *not* to be like the Pharisees. He reminded them that the Pharisees "love the uppermost rooms at feasts, and the chief seats in the synagogues. And greetings in the markets, and to be called of men, Rabbi, Rabbi. But be not ye called Rabbi: for one is your Master, even Christ; and all ye are brethren. And call no man your father upon the earth: for one is your Father, which is in heaven. Neither be ye called masters: for one is your Master, even Christ."

With that exhortation from Jesus, John's disciples were wrong in calling John the Baptist Rabbi. Notice that Jesus emphasized His admonition by repeating it: "Don't be called rabbi or master because there is only one Master, and I am that Master."

Nicodemus made another remarkable confession: "*We know* that thou art a teacher *come from God.*" From this statement, we might assume that all of the Sanhedrin Council knew who Jesus was but chose to reject Him. Remember what John said: "He came unto his own, and his own received him not" (John1:11).

The Pharisees were what we would call in today's world "the apostasy." These are people who know who Jesus Christ is but reject His authority in their lives. They deny His lordship. After all, those who know without a doubt that Jesus is the Son of God, the angels that fell, "believe and tremble" (James 2:19). These angels would legitimately be called apostate angels.

The Pharisees wanted that authority for themselves. Isn't that just like the apostates of today? They want to apply the authority of Almighty God to themselves. Notice that Nicodemus did not say, "We *think* thou art a teacher come from God," but rather that "we *know* thou art a teacher come from God." In other words, Nicodemus was confessing that Jesus came from Heaven—the abode of God—and admitting that the rest of the Sanhedrin believed it, too.

Think about it! Isn't that exactly what happened to Adam and Eve in the Garden of Eden? When the serpent persuaded Eve to eat the fruit of the tree of the knowledge of good and evil, he said, "God doth know that in the day ye eat thereof, then your eyes shall be opened, ye shall be as gods, knowing good and evil" (Genesis 3:5). In other words, he was telling her that God was deceiving her, trying to keep her under His power and authority, wanting to have all of the power in His hands. Satan convinced her that by denying God's authority, she would have it for herself. That's just what those who reject Christ today think: "Why should I give my life, my independence, my power to do what I want to do, to God. Let God run the lives of the weak and beggarly. I can handle myself, thank you." Of course, Adam and Eve brought death and chaos upon themselves and the rest of creation! What will happen to the "authority" of those who deny Christ as their Lord, their Master, when they die? Who will have all of the authority then? Jesus said, "Whosoever therefore shall confess me before men, him will I confess also before my Father which is in heaven. But whosoever shall deny me before men, him will I also deny before my Father which is in heaven" (Matthew

7

10:32–33). Take note that He said absolutely nothing about accepting Him as your Savior. In fact, of all the doctrines of the evangelical churches, that is one that is not mentioned anywhere in the Bible!

Anyone who truly believes that the Bible is the Word of God would have to take the Lord Jesus Christ at His word. He told His disciples, "Ye call me Master and Lord: and ye say well; for so I am" (John 13:13). Have you ever considered the ramifications of what that statement means for you? Do you call Jesus *Master and Lord*, or do you reject His authority as Adam and Eve did? If the latter is the case, are you willing to become a castaway? That is, in fact, what happened to Adam and Eve. They were cast out of the garden of Eden and were never allowed back.

It is no coincidence that the very first sermon that was preached on the day of Pentecost—the birthday of the Church—the Apostle Peter made this declaration: "For David is not ascended into the heavens but he saith himself, The Lord said unto my Lord, Sit thou on my right hand, Until I make thy foes thy footstool. Therefore let all the house of Israel know assuredly, that *God hath made that same Jesus*, whom ye have crucified, *both Lord and Christ*" (Acts 2:34–36).

Hebrews 10:38–39 gives this warning: "Now the just shall live by faith: But if any man draw back, my soul shall find no pleasure in him. But we are not of them who draw back [turn their backs] unto perdition [damnation]; but of them that believe to the saving of the soul." We are given a choice: Christ and His kingdom or the world and its eternal judgment. If we choose Christ, we place ourselves under His authority. He is our Lord. If we turn

our backs on Him and reject His authority, then we face
an eternal hell.

He Is Lord!

And why call ye me, Lord
Lord, and do not the things
which I say? **[Luke 6:46]**

Isn't it ironic that not only was the Edenic couple the first people on Earth and the first to be selected by God to care for His creation, but they were also the first apostates? They believed in God, but they chose to reject His authority. James 2:19 reminds us that "the devils also believe and tremble." They also defected from Christ, thinking they could rise above Him and His authority.

The Bible teaches that there will be a great defection from Christ (apostates) in the last days. This brings us to 2 Thessalonians 2:3, "Let no man deceive you by any means: for that day [the day of the Lord—the time labeled by some people as the tribulation] shall not come except there come a falling away [Greek: *apostasia*] first, and that man of sin be revealed, the son of perdition." I believe we are living in that time-frame, the age of apostasy, in which the churches will be crowded with people who call themselves Christians, but who reject the lordship of Christ!

Never forget that it is our confession that Christ is Lord, our supreme and final authority, and our belief that He was raised from the dead so that He could be Lord both of the dead and the living that brings us to redemption: "For none of us liveth to himself, and no man dieth to himself. For whether we live, we live unto the Lord; and whether we die, we die unto the Lord: whether we live therefore, or die, we are the Lord's. For to this end [*for this reason*] Christ both

10

died, and rose, and revived, *that he might be Lord* both of the dead and living" (Romans 14:7–9).

First Corinthians 15:1–5 specifies this as the gospel of our salvation: "Moreover, brethren, I declare unto you the gospel, which also I preached unto you, which also ye have received, and wherein ye stand; By which also ye are saved, if ye keep in memory what I preached unto you, unless ye have believed in vain; For I delivered unto you first of all that which I also received, how that Christ died for our sins according to the Scriptures; And that he was buried, and that he rose again the third day according to the Scriptures; And that he was seen." This is the same gospel presented in Romans 14 that tells us that the reason for this gospel is so that Jesus Christ "might be Lord both of the dead and living!"

Adam and Eve rebelled against the Lord. Their rebellion resulted in the fall of God's creation and the fall of man to the bondage of sin and death. The Lord Jesus Christ chose to come to this earth in the form of a man to redeem man from his sins. In so doing, the Son of God, Lord of lords, and King of kings suffered extreme humiliation, pain, and death on a Roman cross, shedding His blood so that every man, woman, and child could be saved from everlasting punishment for their rebellion against the Lord of glory—even for those who think they are wiser than God. We are all given the choice to serve the Lord Jesus Christ, thereby winning eternal life, or to serve our own pitiful ambitions without Christ, thereby earning eternal damnation.

Just pause for a moment and think about it. If Christ created us, if God the Father declared Him to be God and Lord of that creation, and if our life on earth and for all eternity depends upon Him, how can we not recognize the fact that He owns us—lock, stock, and barrel? He is our Lord, and He has the total authority to decide what He will or will not do with us.

Jesus told His disciples, "All power is given unto me in heaven and in earth" (Matthew 28:18). How much power is given to Christ? All of it! There is no power or authority in the entire realm of God that exceeds that of Christ. At the throne of Almighty God, Jesus has *all* of the power because *all* power is given to Him in Heaven. The earth is His to do with as He pleases because *all* power is given to Him in Earth. Who are we in all of God's creation to reject that authority, that power?

Yet there are still those who fight over this very issue. They deny the relevance of the Lordship of Christ to the salvation experience. They claim that it relegates our salvation to *our* works when just the opposite is true. Our salvation depends entirely upon *His* works. If that were not true, He could not be Lord at all! There is no "work" involved in our turning our lives over to Christ. God is the one who sets the rules, not we pitiful, lowly people. We think we know more than God. We think we can tell God what He may or may not require for our salvation or, for that matter, how we live our lives.

It is to the contrary of those who deny the necessity of our confession of His Lordship—it is a doctrine of *commitment to Christ*. If you are one who denies this Biblical truth, then ask yourself this question: According to Romans 14:9, why did Christ die, rise from the dead, and live again? If your answer is anything less than "so He might be *Lord* both of the dead and living," then you are less than honest with yourself and with Almighty

God. You would simply deny that the Bible is the Word of God.

In this same passage, Romans 14:8, we are told that we belong to the Lord—"We are the Lord's." In 1 Corinthians 6:20, Paul explains why this is true, "For ye are bought with a price [the precious blood of Jesus Christ]: therefore glorify God in your body, and in your spirit, *which are God's.*" He repeats the thought in 7:22–23: "For he that is called in the Lord, being a servant, is the Lord's freeman: likewise also he that is called, being free, is *Christ's servant.* Ye are bought with a price; be not ye servants of men." In Ephesians 1:13–14 we see that "ye were sealed with that holy Spirit of promise, Which is the earnest of our inheritance until the day of redemption of the purchased possession, unto the praise of his glory."

You see, the Gospel, which is our salvation, rests entirely upon who He is and how we relate to Him. The reason Christ died, was buried, and rose again was to establish for us the fact that He is our Lord! Without that Lordship, Christ does not have the power or authority to save us from sin and redeem us to Himself! By rejecting His Lordship, we deny Him that authority.

Romans 10:9–10 informs us "that if thou shalt confess with thy mouth Jesus as Lord [the literal translation], and shalt believe in thine heart that God hath raised him from the dead, thou shalt be saved. For with the heart man believeth unto righteousness; and with the mouth confession is made *unto salvation.*"

Since Jesus said in Matthew 10:32, "Whosoever therefore shall confess me before men, him will I confess also before my Father which is in heaven. But whosoever shall deny me before men, him will I deny before my Father which is in heaven," what is it that we must confess? *Jesus Christ is Lord!* But verbal expressions alone aren't enough. In this same chapter, Jesus explains Himself: "He that loveth father or mother more than me is not worthy of me: and he that loveth son or daughter more than me is not worthy of me. And he that taketh not his cross, and followeth after me, is not worthy of me. He that findeth his life shall lose it: and he that loseth his life *for my sake* shall find it" (Matthew 10:37–39).

One perfect example of our Lord's declaration is that of missionaries Nate Saint, Jim Elliot, Ed McCully, Roger Youderian, and Peter Fleming— missionaries who were massacred by Auca Indians in South America years ago. Elizabeth Elliot and Rachel Saint went back to the same Indians and led many of them to Christ. That is total commitment to Christ—both for the men who willingly gave their lives for the cause of Christ and for the women who loved the Aucas enough to risk their own lives! And why would they do that? Because they took up the cross and followed the Lord.

You might say, "But they were missionaries. Missionaries often run into trouble." I guess you would be right. Apart from the Lord Jesus Christ, the Apostle Paul was the first missionary, and he certainly did run into trouble. But then you are also called to be a missionary, "For even hereunto were ye called: because Christ also suffered for us, leaving us an example, that ye should follow his steps" (1 Peter 2:21).

Christ is the example for everyone who commits his or her life to Him, everyone who is truly a child of God. He suffered for you and me, and He expects no less from us. We are expected to follow in His steps. Remember the words of Jesus: "And he that taketh not his cross, and followeth after me, is not worthy of me."

Luke expressed the same truth that we saw in Matthew 10. But Luke takes a slightly different approach. In Luke 9:23–26, Jesus said, "If any man will come after me, let him deny himself, and take up his cross *daily,* and follow me. For whosoever will save his life shall lose it: but whosoever will lose his life *for my sake*, the same shall save it. For what is a man advantaged, if he gain the whole world, and lose himself, or be cast away? For whosoever shall be ashamed of me and of my words, of him shall the Son of man be ashamed, when he shall come in his own glory, and in his Father's, and of the holy angels."

Are You Acceptable?

*To the praise of his grace, wherein he
hath made us accepted in the beloved.
In whom we have redemption through
his blood, the forgiveness of sins,
according to the riches of his grace.*
[Ephesians 1:6–7]

The churches in America are often limited by people
who seem to think that going to Heaven is dependent
only on whether or not they claim to be Christians.
Throughout my travels, I have asked a number of people
whether or not they were Christians who responded in
the affirmative, and yet they didn't know anything about
Christ or the Bible. The plain truth is that if you call a
donkey a horse it is still a donkey.

Sad to say. many pastors are of the opinion that most
people who attend church services in America are probably "donkeys!" These are people who use the church
as a crutch for their failure to commit themselves to following Christ. They use church membership, baptism,
Sunday School attendance, tithing their money, and any
number of activities they think will satisfy their quest for
eternal life. But if that's what you think, you won't buy a
nickel's worth of Heaven!

There is a doctrine that has been held for many de-
cades dating back to the late nineteenth century, that may
well have been a contributing factor to an apparent de-
cline in the spirituality of many congregations. For lack
of a better title, I call it the doctrine of "the acceptability
of Christ." A. W. Tozer often referred to it as "a divided

Christ." You have no doubt heard preachers give invitations on Christ's behalf by saying things like, "It's as simple as ABC. All you have to do is accept Christ as your Savior, and you are immediately saved!"

While I attended the Moody Graduate School, I sat under an instructor who had just written a small book titled: *Lordship Salvation, Is It Biblical*? In the book, he rejects everything I've said thus far. He rejects the need for repentance since repentance requires a turning away from sin. He complains that those who believe you must confess Christ as Lord deny the free gift of God and quotes part of what Paul told the Philippian jailer in Acts 16:31, "Believe on the Lord Jesus Christ and thou shalt be saved [omitting 'and thy house']. What he fails to say, however, is that one must believe on [again meaning commit oneself to] the *Lord* Jesus Christ. In the classroom this instructor said the word Lord simply means "Mister," and all that one really needs to do is accept Christ as his or her Savior.

That makes a mockery of Almighty God. Let me remind you of what Peter announced on the birthday of the Church, the day of Pentecost, "Therefore let all the house of Israel know assuredly, that *God hath made that same Jesus*, whom ye have crucified, *both Lord and Christ*" (Acts 2:36).

Let me explain my understanding of what the Scriptures teach regarding the notion that we must find Christ acceptable in order to receive eternal life. Whoops! I'm sorry. The Scriptures teach *nothing* about this subject. I don't think the King of kings, Creator of the universe, and Author of our salvation is somehow impressed by whether or not we find His offer of salvation acceptable. The Lord

17

of glory doesn't need to be grateful for our favor. The problem I see with the phrase "accepting Christ" is that it can't be defined apart from the definition I have assumed it to mean. Otherwise, what other meaning could it possibly have?

Oh, I know that some argue that it has just become a catchword for the decision to become a Christian, but that, of course, makes it a doctrine of salvation by works—a work of self-determination! It's like saying, "I have decided that I am going to Heaven." Such a condition, in itself, will cause many to assume they are going to Heaven, when the opposite may be true. One's relationship with God is determined by one's commitment to Christ as Lord.

Second, as I said earlier, there is no Scriptural reference for the term. As I study God's Word, I have an overriding rule that I follow faithfully. When it comes to spiritual matters, if it isn't in the Bible, it isn't true! The idea of simply "accepting Christ as your Savior" is *not* in the Bible! Some will say that it's just another way of saying "believe in the Lord Jesus Christ." That doesn't hold a drop of water because almost every use of the word "believe" in the New Testament means "to commit yourself to" or "to have faith in." One exception has to do with the devils or demons. James 2:19 tells us that "the devils also believe [in one God], and tremble."

In John 2:23–24, we are given an account of those who were in Jerusalem to celebrate the passover feast. We are told that "many believed in his name, when they saw the miracles which he did. But Jesus did not *commit* himself unto them, because he knew all men." In this verse the word *commit* is the same Greek word that is most often translated *believe*. In those cases, the translation is "to have faith in." In other words, Jesus did not trust those Jews who outwardly believed in His name because of the miracles they had witnessed. It was a false "belief" on their part to the name of Christ, and Jesus would not commit Himself to them in any way.

How often I have heard a well-meaning believer tell someone that "all you need to do is accept Christ as your Savior," and then have that person repeat a prayer making that statement. Afterward, the would-be evangelist pronounces the person "saved." That "saved" person then goes merrily along in sin, never having either a personal relationship with Christ or a commitment to Him! Words alone don't save souls!

Only a heart-felt commitment to Christ as your Lord will do that. It's an act of confession, contrition, and repentance from sin. You'll notice that I did not include "works of righteousness." You can't be saved through baptism, tithing, church membership, or even "good behavior," because "we are all as an unclean thing, and all our righteousnesses are as filthy rags; and we all do fade as a leaf; and our iniquities, like the wind, have taken us away" (Isaiah 64:6)."

Nor can you be saved by declaring Christ to be acceptable to you! It's amazing that so many people believe in the "accept Christ" doctrine of salvation and label any other viewpoint as "salvation by works." Salvation comes by way of the gift of God's grace. We cannot save ourselves. If I were to say that I'm saved because *I* accepted *Christ* and not because Christ accepted me, that means that I saved myself. In other words, it places our salvation under our own control, our own authority, instead of God's authority. Our role is to believe what He has done for us and yield our lives to Him. What did God do to provide us with His grace? What gracious act did He perform? He sacrificed His only begotten Son on Calvary's cross! The shed blood of Jesus Christ was provided for us by way of God's grace! Then He raised Him from the dead. That's something that no one else could do. The grace of God is "not of yourselves: it is the gift of God" (Ephesians 2:8).

I have been reminded that since salvation is a gift from God, in order to receive that gift you have to accept it. Otherwise, it never really belongs to you. But that simply is not the case. When I was a child, Christmas was an exciting day for our family of ten. The children would leap from their beds and hurry to the Christmas tree and gaze in awe at the gifts. Each child usually had one or two presents lying under or near the tree, and we found it hard to wait to open them. At a given signal, we looked for the packages with each of our names on them. We didn't have to accept the gifts because they were already ours. After all, they had our names attached to them. Mom would say, "Those are Larry's gifts over there," and I would immediately grab them and tear the paper from the packages. I suppose one could say that Mom and Dad found me acceptable enough to give me the gifts of their own free will. The gifts were free indeed, and they belonged to me before I even knew where or what they were! When we confess Christ as our Lord with our heart by faith, the gift of eternal life automatically belongs to us! Our Lord purchased it for us and put our names on it!

Of course, Christ is never referred to in the Bible as a gift. That's an assumption based on an incorrect approach to "dividing the word." In John 3:16 eternal life is the gift as the result of Christ offering Himself as a sacrificial Lamb. He is, instead, the gift Giver.

Now there are only three verse references in the New Testament that refer to a free gift. Romans 5:15–17. These verses refer to the free *gift of righteousness* that is given to a believer. Verse 17 says, "For if by one man's offence death reigned by one; much more they which receive abundance of grace and of *the gift of righteousness* shall reign in life by one, Jesus Christ." In this case, two gifts are referred to: the gift of the abundance of grace and the gift of righteousness. The Greek word translated "gift" in the Authorized version literally means *an endowment—something the Giver freely chooses to give.* An endowment is something that can be measured as in Ephesians 4:7, "But unto every one of us [every believer] is given grace according to the measure of the gift of Christ [or the gift that Christ gives]." In other words, Christ bestows a measure of grace to every believer as He chooses. That's why Paul called it the "abundance of grace." That's a measurable amount.

Ephesians 2: 8–9 presents another gift, a gift of spiritual protection: "For by grace are ye saved [*kept safe* or *protected*] through faith; and that not of yourselves, it is the gift of God: Not of works, lest any man should boast." In this case, there is a variation in the Greek. The word *gift* means *a sacrificial offering*—that is, the sacrifice Christ made of Himself. Our security is freely presented to us as the result of the shed blood of Christ. The safety or security of a born again believer, those of us who have been "quickened together" (Ephesians 2:5), is the subject. Jesus promised us, "I will never leave thee, nor forsake thee. So that we may boldly say, The Lord is my helper, and I will not fear what man shall do unto me" (Hebrews 13:5–6). Why? Because Ephesians 2:10 tells us that "we are his workmanship, created in Christ Jesus unto good works, which God hath before ordained that we should walk in them." We are re-created for a purpose beyond our salvation, and that is to fulfill an ordination to do good works.

Ephesians 3:1–2 tells us that Paul was given, or gifted, the dispensation [*administration*] of grace. In this case, grace is presented to Paul to pass along to the Gentile believers at Ephesus. "For this cause I Paul, the prisoner of Jesus Christ for you Gentiles, If ye have heard of the dispensation of the grace of God which is given me to you-ward . . . ." Paul was assigned the administration of the knowledge of God's grace to the Gentiles.

Finally, we are told that "the wages of sin is death; but the gift of God is *eternal life* through Jesus Christ our Lord" (Romans 6:23). Once again, the word gift refers to a *spiritual endowment*. Hence, God gives gifts freely to us—gifts of grace, righteousness, security, and eternal life.

Romans 5:21 states, "As sin hath reigned unto death, even so might *grace* reign through *righteousness* [*holiness*] unto eternal life by Jesus Christ our Lord." Isn't it interesting that the measure of the gift of grace that is meted out to us is based on the strength of our righteousness or holiness? Notice that Paul is talking about the two free gifts, grace and righteousness, as well as the gift of eternal life. This verse makes the difference between the effects sin has upon us and that of turning from sin to serve the Lord. A life in sin without repentance results in death—specifically the second death, the lake of fire—while living for Christ results in the rewards of eternal life.

We don't need to play word-games when it comes to the most important issue to any human soul. We don't need to create fanciful techniques or phrases in order to coax a lost soul to Christ. We need to tell it like it really is! Salvation is based on your commitment to and not your acceptance of the Giver. You are literally trading your life and soul for a new life in Christ. Christ, the Son of God, died an agonizing death on the cross. He paid a great price for the salvation He has offered to you. The price He paid was the purchase price for your commitment to Him. He gave you His life expecting you to give Him yours! You see, you are not accepting Christ, you are committing your life to Him for who He is and what he did to offer you eternal life. The plain and simple truth is that you cannot accept or possess Christ as your Savior without first confessing Him as your Lord. God said so! Every epistle in the New Testament is a guideline for following Christ in a life of obedience to Him. The Gospels are replete with instructions to follow Christ. In John 10:27–28 Jesus said, "My sheep hear my voice, and I know them, and they follow me: And I give unto them eternal life; and they shall never perish, neither shall any man pluck them out of my hand."

Ephesians 1:6 tells us that it is "to the praise of the glory of *his grace*, wherein *he* hath made *us* accepted in the beloved." In fact, it is not possible to come to Christ without being drawn to Him. Jesus said, "No man can come to me, except the Father which hath sent me draw him: and I will raise him up at the last day" (John 6:44).

23

It is not the other way around. Our Lord does not want us to *accept* Him; He wants us to *commit* ourselves to Him. Colossians 3:23–24 exhorts us, "And whatsoever ye do, do it heartily, as to the Lord, and not unto men. Knowing that of the Lord ye shall receive the reward of the inheritance: for ye serve the Lord Christ."

Confessing Christ as your Lord is not based on your works. Your works are based on your commitment to Him as your Lord. Paul tells us in 2 Corinthians 5:17, "Therefore if any man be in Christ, he is a new creature; old things have passed away; behold, all things are become new." Hence, if you are *in Christ*, you are a new creation, you are *His workmanship*, and you are created in Christ to *do good works* according to Ephesians 2:10. In fact, we are *ordained* by God to walk in those good works. It is to be our life-long activity. Why? Because the One who re-created us is our Lord, and we must obey Him. After all, that's why He re-created us.

By the way, there is nothing wrong with the word "obey." Romans 6:16 makes it clear: "Know ye not, that to whom ye yield yourselves servants to obey, his servants ye are to whom ye obey; whether of sin unto death, or of obedience unto righteousness?" We have a choice. We can obey the Lord Jesus Christ, thereby gaining eternal life, or we can remain in our old sinful state and perish in it.

"Aha!" some might say, "You do believe you are saved by works if you have to obey Him!" My dad's response would have been, "Hogwash!" The writer of Hebrews said, "Though he [Christ] were a Son, yet learned he obedience by the things which he suffered; And being made perfect, he became the author of eternal salvation unto all them that obey him" (Hebrews 5:8–9). I will readily admit that obedience to the Lord is not always comfortable, nor is it always devoid of work. After all, Philippians 2:7–8 describes the obedience of God's Son, the King of kings and Lord of lords, who "made himself of no reputation , and took upon him the form of a servant, and was made in the likeness of men: And being found in fashion as a man, he humbled himself, and became obedient unto death, even the death of the cross." Pity the man who would talk about obedience as though it were a crime for Almighty God to demand less of us or that somehow it would reflect poorly on his reputation.

A New and Living Way:

Having therefore, brethren, boldness to enter into the holiest by the blood of Jesus, By a new and living way, which he hath consecrated for us, through the vail, that is to say, his flesh; And having a high priest over the house of God; Let us draw near with a true heart in full assurance of faith, having our hearts sprinkled from an evil conscience, and our bodies washed with pure water. **[Hebrews 10:19–22]**

We often misconstrue the phrase "not of works" in Ephesians 2:9, thinking that it means that you don't have to *do* anything to be saved. In other words, we can be lazy to the nth degree and just sit back and say, "Here I am, you lucky God. Take me, but please don't use me. Don't expect me to do anything on your behalf."

In Acts 16:30, the Philippian jailor asked Paul, "What must I *do* to be saved? Then Paul proceeded to tell him what to *do*. "Believe on the Lord Jesus Christ, and thou shalt be saved, and thy house" (31). Rarely do we hear anyone explain what the phrase "believe on" means. The Greek that is translated "believe on" is the word *pisteuo* or *pistis,* and it means "commit yourself to." So if you believe on the Lord Jesus Christ, you are committed to Him; and if you are not committed to Him, you are not saved.

When we talk about confession, we usually assume that we are to confess our sins to the Lord, and that is certainly a part of confession. David prayed, "I acknowledged my sin unto thee, and mine iniquity have I not hid.

26

I said, I will confess my transgressions unto the Lord; and thou forgavest the iniquity of my sin" (Psalm 32:5).

John said, "If we confess our sins, he is faithful and just to forgive our sins, and to cleanse us from all unrighteousness" (1 John 1:9). When we confess our sins, God forgives us. We certainly can't forgive our own sins. Only God can do that! Then God cleanses us from all unrighteousness. Again, we can't cleanse ourselves. Only God can do that!

This type of confession requires not only acknowledging that we are sinners, but it requires repentance for the sin that has prevailed in our lives. I recently heard a nationally acclaimed radio preacher declare that "you don't have to repent to be saved; just accept Christ." This man, a former pastor of a very large church, has published Bible study books and CDs containing years of radio sermons, yet he seems oblivious to all the scriptures that exhort people to repent for salvation.

After His resurrection Jesus told His disciples in Luke 24:46–47, "Thus it is written, and thus it behoved Christ to suffer, and to rise from the dead the third day: And that repentance and remission of sins should be preached in his name among all nations, beginning at Jerusalem."

The word *repentance* is similar to the word *conversion*. "Repentance" means to turn our way of *thinking* around, while "conversion" means to turn our way of *living* around. Paul said in Philippians 2:5, "Let this *mind* be in you, which was also in Christ Jesus." That new mind-set can only take place when we have confessed our sins to the Lord and allowed Him to forgive us and cleanse the sins from our hearts.

Paul said in Colossians 3:10 that we have "put on the new man, which is *renewed in knowledge* after the image of him that created him." The word translated "renewed" means to *renovate* or *make new* or *clean up*. We are told that the new man has cleaned-up his way of thinking so it is like the One who created him. In other words, if you have repented and been converted, become a new man, then your thinking and way of living will be Christ-centered. That's what Paul meant when he said, "Let this mind be in you, which was also in Christ Jesus."

Peter told the Jews at Pentecost to "repent" for the "remission of sins." That's something you must *do* to be saved. He said in Acts 3:19, "Repent [turn your way of thinking around] ye therefore, and be converted [turn your way of living around], that your sins may be blotted out, when the times of refreshing shall come from the presence of the Lord." Notice that repentance had to precede conversion. If you don't repent of your sins, your sins will not be expunged, you will not be converted, and you will not be saved. On the other hand, if you have been converted, then you have changed your way of life from that of following after sin to that of following after Christ!

In Philippians 4:7–9, Paul tells us that "the peace of God, which passeth all understanding, shall keep your *hearts and minds* through Christ Jesus. Finally brethren, whatsoever things are true, whatsoever things are honest, whatsoever things are just, whatsoever things are pure, whatsoever things are lovely, whatsoever things are of good report; if there be any praise, *think on these things*. Those things, which ye have both learned, and received, and heard, and seen in me, *do*: and the God of peace shall be with you."

Notice, Paul said that when you *do* the things he listed, then "the God of peace shall be with you." That means that if you don't do them, the God of peace will not be with you. While the peace of God keeps our hearts and minds through Christ Jesus, that peace—the peace that passes understanding—is not available if the God of peace is not with us!

Confession brings peace of mind, primarily because we know that when we have "made a clean breast of things" with the Lord, He has forgiven and washed away the things that have weighed us down with guilt and shame. David said in Psalm 34:18, "The Lord is nigh unto them that are of a broken heart; and saveth such as be of a contrite spirit." You'll notice that "the peace of God, which passeth all understanding" can only be ours when we have allowed the Lord Jesus to be the safe haven for our hearts and minds. The word translated "*keep*" in verse 7 means *to watch over* or *preserve.* That's what Christ does for us when we have confessed our sins to Him. That's what brings the peace of God to our hearts and minds—because we know beyond a doubt that we have found true forgiveness.

Having said all of these things, I do not mean to imply that a Christian will never again have to deal with sin. We still live in a body of flesh, and we will still be tempted by the things of the world. That's why Paul wrote in Colossians 3:1–3, "If ye then be risen with Christ, seek those things which are above, where Christ sitteth on the right hand of God. Set your affections on things above, not on things on the earth. For ye are dead [referring to our being dead to sin], and your life is hid with Christ in God."

We do have this reassurance in 1 Corinthians 10:13, "There hath no temptation taken you but such as is common to man: but God is faithful, who will not suffer you to be tempted above that ye are able; but will with the temptation also make a way to escape, that ye may be able to bear it."

However, when we have allowed ourselves to fall into temptation, we still have the knowledge delivered by John in 1 John 1:9, an admonition that was directed to Christian believers: "If we confess our sins, he is faithful and just to forgive us our sins, and to cleanse us from all unrighteousness."

Then Paul gives another purpose for confession when he said in Romans 10:9–10, "that if thou shalt confess [*acknowledge* or *agree fully*] with thy mouth Jesus as Lord, and shalt *believe in thine heart* that God has raised him from the dead, thou shalt be saved. For *with the heart* man believeth unto *righteousness*; and with the mouth confession is made unto salvation."

The verbal confession to other people that you believe with your heart that Jesus Christ is your Lord, proved to you by His resurrection, opens the door to the commitment you make. You see, His resurrection establishes the fact that He is the Lord of life itself, and when we acknowledge that fact to other people we also acknowledge that He is the Lord of our own lives!

That's why Paul added in verse 11, "For the scripture saith, Whosoever believeth on him shall not be ashamed." And that's why Jesus said in Matthew 10:32–33, "Whosoever therefore shall *confess me before men*, him will I confess also before my Father which is in heaven. But whosoever shall deny me before men, him will I also deny before my Father which is in heaven."

Knowing these things, you can understand why confessing Christ as our Lord is absolutely essential for our salvation. It has nothing to do with works, but rather it has everything to do with commitment. After all, why should Christ have committed Himself to us by the way of the cross if we are not willing to commit ourselves to Him by the same way.

As I said before, the idea of "accepting Christ as your Savior" is not in the Bible. In fact, just the opposite is true. *He* must find *you* acceptable to *Him*. Romans 12:1 and 2 exemplifies what God expects of us: "I beseech you therefore, brethren, by the mercies of God, that you present your bodies a living [Greek: *a life of*] sacrifice, holy, acceptable unto God, which is your reasonable service. And be not conformed to this world: but be ye transformed by the renewing of your mind, that ye may approve what is that good, and acceptable, and perfect, will of God." In other words, what God deems good and acceptable constitutes His perfect will. I often hear people ask, "How can I know the will of God?" Let's examine the subject since our Lord clearly wants you to know what His will is for you.

First, He tells us to present our bodies a living and holy sacrifice. In 1 Peter 3:15–18 we are told to "sanctify the Lord God in your hearts." That means we are be partakers of His holiness and His purity in order to consecrate our hearts to Him. Being sanctified by the presence of God in your heart is accomplished by your yielding to the Holy Spirit and enables you to "be ready always to give an answer to every man that asketh you a reason of the hope that is in you with meekness and fear. Having a good conscience; that, whereas they speak evil of you, as of evil doers, they may be ashamed that falsely accuse your good conversation [*behavior*] in Christ."

If you are truly a child of God, born of and sanctified by the Holy Spirit, then you must act like it. Romans 12:1 tells us that this is acceptable and reasonable. That means that anything else is neither acceptable nor reasonable. It stands to reason that if presenting our bodies holy and living sacrifices is acceptable to God, then if we fail to do so, it is *un*acceptable to God. If doing so is also our *reasonable* service, then our failure to do so is *un*reasonable.

We are to give our *lives* to the cause of Christ. Examine your own life. How much of your time, possessions, and energy do you spend for the Lord? How much do you suffer as a result of it? You might ask, "Does that mean that we have to suffer for Christ?" Paul tells us in Romans 8:16–18, "The Spirit himself beareth witness with our spirit, that we are the children of God: And if children, then heirs; heirs of God, and joint-heirs with Christ; *if so be that we suffer with him*, that we may be also glorified together. For I reckon that the sufferings of this present time are not worthy to be compared with the glory which shall be revealed in us."

Then we are instructed to "be not conformed to this world." John tells us in 1 John 2:15–17, "Love not the world, neither the things that are in the world. If any man love the world, the love of the Father is not in him. For all that is in the world, the lust of the flesh, and the lust of the eyes, and the pride of life, is not of the Father, but is of the world. And the world passeth away, and the lust thereof: but he that doeth *the will of God* abideth forever." By not conforming to this world, by renewing our minds [turning our way of thinking around] , and by living holy and sacrificial lives for the cause of Christ constitute the good and acceptable, and perfect will of God.

People often tend to read these verses from Romans 12 with what seems like a tongue-in-cheek attitude—especially those who stand in the pulpit and fail to fully explain the text which is more often than not the case. In the event one thinks that sitting on a hard pew and getting a crick in the back constitutes sacrificial living, he is from another world. Verse one states that if we are to receive the mercies of God, then we must present our bodies a living sacrifice. The Greek word for sacrifice literally means *to breathe hard* or *to smoke as by fire.* Even Webster's New World Dictionary gives two primary definitions. The predominant definition is the one exemplified in the Old Testament where animals are killed and burned on the altar (or the blood being sprinkled on the Mercy Seat); a physical sacrifice to honor God. It does not mean simply doing without something we want or think we need. The other definition given in the dictionary is that of a baseball play in which a player on base is "sacrificed over to another base." The fact is the player doing the sacrifice is put out. He loses his turn at bat.

What does this have to do with our bodies? It's quite simple. When we suffer, our bodies are the first to feel it, but it goes beyond pain. We can suffer without physical pain. We are told in 1 Peter 4:1–2, "Forasmuch then as Christ hath suffered for us in the flesh, arm yourselves likewise with the same mind: for he that hath suffered in the flesh hath ceased from sin; That he no longer should live the rest of his time in the flesh to the lusts of men, but to the will of God."

That's where the holiness aspect of Romans 12:1 comes in. "I beseech you therefore, brethren, by the mercies of God, that you present your bodies a living sacrifice, *holy*, acceptable unto God, which is your reasonable service." When we no longer allow the flesh to control us, to reign over our lives, our suffering begins. That's when we will suffer for Christ's sake!

Finally, Romans 12:2 establishes the very foundation of the new birth because you are "*transformed* by the renewing of your mind." That's called conversion, the result of repentance, and through this transformation His will is to deliver you from this present evil world according to Galatians 1:3–4, "Grace be to you and peace from God the Father, and from our Lord Jesus Christ, Who gave himself for our sins, that he might deliver us from this present evil world, *according to the will of God* and our Father."

I get concerned when I hear anyone say that "you don't have to give anything up to be saved. Just accept Christ as your Savior." That is not true! If you don't give your sinful habits up, you have not repented; you have not been converted. I've had people tell me, "I can't live the life. There are too many things I can't change." It seems like some would-be soul-winners are so concerned about winning others to Christ that they get desperate enough to try any ploy to make it as easy as possible, and they cave in to such feeble excuses for rejecting Christ. If you make it sound easy enough, then a lost person will readily say what you want him to say. That way you can boast that you saved another soul. It doesn't work that way!

I once sat under a pastor who preached about his security once he was saved and delighted in saying, "I am secure in my salvation. Now I can do anything I want to." That just isn't true! A Christian lives for Christ. If he just does what *he* wants to, then he is denying the Lordship of Christ. He must do what *the Lord* wants him to. That doesn't mean that he won't fail now and then, but his goal is to emulate Christ. We give up what *we* want to do with our lives the moment we confess Christ as our Lord.

Peter told the Jews at Pentecost, "Unto you first God, having raised up his Son Jesus, sent him to bless you, in turning away every one of you from his iniquities" (Acts 3:26). God gave this message to Solomon, "If my people, which are called by name, shall humble themselves, and pray, and seek my face, and turn from their wicked ways; then will I hear from heaven, and will forgive their sin" (2 Chronicles 7:14). God established His requirements for the forgiveness of sin.

In Hebrews 11:6 we are told, "But without faith it is impossible to please him [*God*]: for he that cometh to God must believe that he is, and that he is a rewarder of them that diligently seek him."

Paul said in Romans 6:22–23, "But now being made free from sin, and become servants to God, ye have your fruit unto holiness, and the end everlasting life. For the wages of sin is death; but the gift of God is eternal life through Jesus Christ our Lord." It's odd that some people love to quote 6:23, but never 6:22. Since we have become servants to God, His Lordship over us is established. There is no such thing as a servant without a Lord! Paul states emphatically that everlasting life is based on our being made free from sin and made servants of God. This is what gives us the ability to have "fruit unto holiness."

If one continues to allow sin to reign in his body, the wages of that sin is still death. A Christian has turned his life over to Christ so that Christ will reign in and over him. We can't have it both ways. Jesus said, "No servant can serve two masters: for either he will hate the one, and love the other; or else he will hold to the one, and despise the other. Ye cannot serve God and mammon" (Luke 16:13). In Mark 3:25, He said, "And if a house be divided against itself, that house cannot stand."

It was in *this* context that Jesus went on to say, "Verily I say unto you, All sins shall be forgiven unto the sons of men, and blasphemies wherewith soever they shall blaspheme. But he that shall blaspheme against the Holy Ghost hath never forgiveness, but is in danger of eternal damnation" (Mark 3:28–29).

Have you ever wondered what it means to "blaspheme against the Holy Ghost?" Think about it! It's that old "house divided against itself." It's having it both ways—trying to serve two masters—claiming to serve the Lord Jesus Christ and maintaining a servant relationship to sin! You will never be forgiven until you choose to allow Christ to reign over you because the wages of sin is death. You must choose which lord you will serve— Satan or Christ, the reign of sin or the reign of "fruit unto holiness."

I heard a preacher confess to one of his church members that he had launched into the man in a venomous tirade, then later apologized, stating that he had allowed Satan into his heart to control him. That's the old house divided against itself. His statement exposed the fact that this preacher was not a regenerate man, since the Spirit of God would not, and could not, share the inner man with Satan.

The preacher in question gradually began to tear down the church by treating other members the same way and chasing some away. He stole money from the church and became lavish with spending the church's money on things they couldn't afford. Then he began to pit members against each other. When the deacons confronted the preacher, his reaction was to declare that they couldn't do anything to him because he had only to answer to God. Only God had the authority to remove him from the church. That's where every cult begins! The next step would be for such a man to declare that he is equal with God and then very God. That's exactly what caused Lucifer's fall, and it's what caused the serpent to persuade Eve to seek the same power. Satan wields a heavy sword, and the church accepted the preacher's raving. They didn't realize that Christ wields a heavier sword—one that is "quick, and powerful, and sharper than any two-edged sword, piercing even to the dividing asunder of soul and spirit, and of the joints and marrow, and is a discerner of the thoughts and intents of the heart" (Hebrews 4:12). Christians don't have to bow to Satan's tyranny because "our God is a consuming fire" (Hebrews 12:29).

There were many complaints about the direction the church had taken, but no one had the spiritual courage or faith enough in God to take the necessary action of removing their "thorn in the flesh." As a result, they caved in to the enemy's onslaught and sought counsel regarding bankruptcy and church closure. They had been robbed of their spiritual backbone along with the financial means to pay their bills. That's what happens when the flock begins to disintegrate—to flee from the adversary rather than face him head-on. The would-be dragon slayers dropped their swords and retreated.

We have so much to contend with in this world. No matter which way we turn, we have three adversaries that are always there to cause us to stumble—the world, the flesh and the devil—and the temptations of today are greater than ever because the end of the age is approaching. But friend, we have something that nothing in this world can overcome. John tells us that "every spirit that confesseth not that Jesus Christ is come in the flesh is not of God: and this is that spirit of antichrist, whereof ye have heard that it should come; and even now already is it in the world. Ye are of God, little children, and have overcome them: because greater is he that is in you, than he that is in the world" (1 John 4:3–4). Notice that *the Holy Spirit is in you* if you are a born-again believer, but Satan is in the world and *not* in you.

For those of us who know the Lord, we know that we have a source of power that is greater than any other force in all the universe dwelling in us in the person of the Holy Spirit. Satan does not, and cannot, indwell us. Because of the indwelling presence of the Spirit of Christ, we can rejoice in the reminder in 1 John:15–17— "Whosoever shall confess that Jesus is the Son of God, God dwelleth in him, and he in God. And we have known and believed the love that God hath to us. God is love; and he that dwelleth in love dwelleth in God, and God in him. Herein is our love made perfect, that we may have boldness in the day of judgment: because as he is, so are we in this world."

So when we fret about the possible suffering we may go through for the cause of Christ, we must keep in mind what He did for us. "For it is better, if the will of God be so, that ye suffer for well doing, than for evil doing. For Christ also hath once suffered for sins, the just for the unjust, that he might bring us to God, being put to death in the flesh, but quickened by the Spirit" (1 Peter 3:17–18).

The writer of Hebrews reminds us of what Jesus did outside the gates of Jerusalem at Calvary: "Wherefore Jesus also, that he might sanctify the people with his own blood, suffered without the gate. Let us go forth therefore unto him without the camp [the way of the cross], bearing his reproach [your sins and mine that He carried to the cross]. For here have we no continuing city, but we seek one to come" (Hebrews 13:12–14).

Contrary to what many preachers are saying today, this present earth will be eradicated, and a new Earth will appear. The Jews look to the earthly Jerusalem, but Christians look for a New Jerusalem that will come down from Heaven to the New Earth.

You see, "in all these things we are more than conquerors through him that loved us. For I am persuaded, that neither death, nor life, nor angels, nor principalities, nor powers, nor things present, nor things to come, Nor height, nor depth, nor any other creature, shall be able to separate us from the love of God, which is in Christ Jesus our Lord" (Romans 8:37–39).

For clarification, let me repeat these basic truths: You cannot save yourself by works of righteousness, not by baptism, church membership, your generosity in giving, your moral standards, or any other action that requires your own initiative. If you choose to "accept Christ" as your Savior, that is a work of your own initiative! It is a declaration that you have selected His saving ability over all other religions, and it is purely an act based on your desire to go to Heaven instead of hell—motivated by total selfishness. In other words, it is tantamount to saying, "If you will assure me of eternal life, then I find that acceptable. If I'm not convinced that you will follow through, then I'll go somewhere else." The simple fact is, no matter how much you search, you will not find anywhere in the Bible where you are told that by accepting Christ as your Savior, you will indeed be saved.

On the other hand, by your relying entirely on the grace of God through His Son, the Lord Jesus Christ, by your faith, you will be saved! What's the difference? Well, under the "acceptance" notion, you are depending upon your personal intellect and your ability to decide whether or not Jesus is trustworthy. For your own convenience, you retain control of everything in your life. God has no say about anything! You have made no promise to give Him a place in your life. You have offered Him absolutely nothing. It's all take and no give, paying the Lord of all creation nothing more than lip service.

However, when you commit your life to Him, *He* assumes control of *your* life and your eternal destiny. As Paul said in 2 Timothy 1:12, "I know whom I have believed, and am persuaded that *he* is able to keep that which I have committed unto him against that day." If He is not the Lord of your life, He does not have the power, the authority, to guarantee your eternity. He has become just one more pawn in your quest to get everything you want for yourself.

Herein is the truth: when we commit our lives to Him, He retains His right to redeem what He has paid for—His purchased possession. If we don't make that commitment, there is no guarantee of our acceptance.

Everything I have said thus far points to the only authority that really matters—our Lord Jesus Christ. Everything that matters in life, we owe to Him. If it does not relate to Him, then it simply doesn't matter in life! Christians, and everything they possess, physically, intellectually, emotionally and spiritually, belong to Him. Our service and every breath we take belongs to Him. Those who reject that basic truth do not belong to Him. They have rejected or denied Him, and therefore, do not have the promise of eternal life because Jesus will deny them (2 Timothy 2:11–12).

Why is it that so many religious people reject some of the most important truths found in the Word of God? Nicodemus was one who recognized the truth when he came face to face with the One who was and is the way, the, truth, and the life. He confessed Jesus as his Master and suggested that the entire Sanhedrin Council believed the same. They were the most powerful men among the religious leadership of the Jews, yet they had set up a system of doctrines and laws that went far beyond what the Scriptures even of their day contained. It has always been the case that human error creeps into many of our commonly held beliefs.

Nicodemus heard what Jesus had to say on that dark night and took Him at His word. He then defended our Lord before the Council in John 7:50, "Nicodemus saith unto them, (he that came to Jesus by night, being one of them,) Doth our law judge a man, before it hear him, and know what he doeth?" When Joseph of Arimathæa, a disciple of Jesus, came to take the body of our Lord from the cross, "there came also Nicodemus, which at first came to Jesus by night, and brought a mixture of myrrh and aloes, about an hundred pound weight. Then took they the body of Jesus, and wound it in linen clothes with the spices, as the manner of the Jews is to bury" (John 19:38–40).

Nicodemus called Jesus, "My Master." My prayer is that you are willing to call Jesus Christ, "My Master," too, confessing Him as the Lord of your life if you haven't already done so.

Examine Yourself:

*Examine yourselves, whether
ye be in the faith; prove your
own selves. Know ye not your
own selves, how that Jesus Christ
is in you, except ye be reprobates?*
[2 Corinthians 13:5]

We've covered a lot of ground in this booklet, but it seems appropriate to recap the basic truths regarding our relationship with the Lord Jesus Christ. We can't have a relationship—we can't have true fellowship—with Christ Jesus, unless we know who He is and what he means to us. John speaks so passionately about our fellowship with our Lord Jesus and with our brothers and sisters in Christ. He makes it a standard for every believer. He said, "That which we have seen and heard declare we unto you, that ye also may have fellowship with us: and truly our fellowship is with the Father, and with his Son Jesus Christ. And these things write we unto you, that your joy may be full" (1 John 1:3–4).

In order to have fellowship with other Christian believers, you must first have fellowship with the Author of every Christian's salvation, the Lord Jesus Christ. There are barriers to that kind of relationship. John said, "that God is light, and in him is no darkness *at all*. If we say we have fellowship with him, and walk in darkness, we lie, and do not the truth" (1 John 1:5–6). When you walk in darkness, you have no opportunity for fellowship of any kind. There is a wall between you and God that all men are prone, not just to build, but to maintain

43

in order to justify their own passions for the things of this world—things that fulfill the desires of the flesh. Of course, the one who is walking in darkness can't even distinguish what that means. His heart and mind are held captive to those things, and like a blind man, he stumbles through life.

As a graduate assistant at the university, one of my responsibilities was to tutor a blind undergraduate student. One experience with him will always stay in my mind. We were seated in his dormitory room as I read the textbook assignment to him, and the phone rang down the hall. The apartment contained several student bedrooms and a lounge.

Paul would have to answer the phone down the hall and around the corner in the lounge area. He insisted on his self-reliance and assured me that he could answer the phone himself. He hurried to his feet and down the hall. As he hurried down the hall I heard a loud thud and the slam of a door. When he returned, he was rubbing his head and said, "I told those guys to always shut their doors because I can't see when they are open!" He had rushed right into a door that another student had left open into the hallway.

I was not used to working with a blind person, and I learned something myself that day. I always checked to make sure his dorm-mates' doors were closed when I went to Paul's room.

You see, when a person is walking in darkness, he has many barriers to stumble into— barriers that stand between him and any potential fellowship with God— open doors designed by Satan to cause him to continually stumble. Those open doors represent temptations to keep him in the darkness of sin. In that darkness, a sinner will either walk through the open doorway to be swallowed up in more paths of darkness, or he will slam into the door and fall backward. Either way, his bondage is assured, and the tighter his bonds are, the more he blames the only Person who can save him from everything that goes wrong—the Lord Jesus Christ.

Anyone who is walking in darkness loves what he knows because he has never seen the Light of life. It seems like a contradiction. He loves his sin, but he hates the pain that results from it. Still he refuses to accept his own responsibility, choosing to accuse the Lord for failing to protect him.

You can't have true fellowship with a stranger. A person who is a stranger to God can only think of God as a stranger to himself. He will be bitter or angry because he doesn't know this stranger called Jesus Christ. He doesn't have access to the privileges that believers have, and when his prayers aren't answered (if, indeed, he prays), then he shakes his fist toward Heaven and curses the holy God whom he doesn't know anything about.

I know of a lady who has declared herself to be an atheist because, in her words, God doesn't answer her prayers. Seems to be a contradiction, doesn't it? She believes enough in God to ask for special favors from Him, but denies His existence because she can't communicate with Him! She is spiritually blind, caught up in the darkness of her own making. Instead of grasping for excuses, she needs to reach out to Jesus, confess her sins, and make Him the Lord of her life.

In order to have the kind of communication that she wants, she has to be in fellowship with Him, but as

John said, "If we say that we have fellowship with him, and walk in darkness, we lie, and do not the truth." It's strange that people want the benefits of God's fellowship but don't want the fellowship itself. How arrogant they are who think they have the right to God's undivided attention when they ignore Him or deny Him at all other times! They would tell us that God doesn't meet their demands when they fall into hard times or get themselves into trouble, but the rest of the time they want God to stay out of their lives and leave them alone. No matter how you peel it, they want to have everything their own way with or without God's help.

The Apostle Paul tells us that there are those who "walk in the vanity of their mind, Having the understanding darkened, being alienated from the life of God through the ignorance that is in them, because of the blindness of their heart" (Ephesians 4:17–18). These are people who choose to maintain their lives in sin and alienate themselves from the very One they want to make demands of. Paul describes the man who walks in the vanity of his mind in Galatians 6:3: "For if a man think himself to be something, when he is nothing, he deceiveth himself." They blindly grope in the darkness of their own making, then accuse God of failing them when things go wrong. How is it that such people can demand things from God while refusing to allow Him into their lives?

John went on to say in 1 John 1:7, "But if we walk in the light, as he is in the light, we have fellowship one with another, and the blood of Jesus Christ his Son cleanseth us from all sin." Aha! That's the proverbial "rub," wanting to "have our cake and eat it, too." But

Jesus made it clear that men love darkness rather than light because their deeds are evil. The only way to fellowship with Him is to confess the sins that have ruled their lives, repent, and confess Christ as the new Lord of their lives. They must know who He is and how He can give them everlasting life.

The first sermon that was preached on the birthday of the Church establishes the importance of the Lordship of Jesus Christ: Acts 2:32–36, "This Jesus hath God raised up, whereof we are all witnesses. Therefore being by the right hand of God *exalted*, and having received of the Father the promise of the Holy Ghost, he hath shed forth this, which ye now see and hear. For David is not ascended into the heavens: but he saith himself, *The Lord said unto my Lord*, Sit thou on my right hand, Until I make thy foes thy footstool. Therefore let all the house of Israel know assuredly, that God hath made that same Jesus, whom ye have crucified, both *Lord and Christ*."

In these verses we see that God the Father calls Jesus Christ *the Lord*! In verse 36 Peter calls Jesus both Lord and Christ [*the Anointed One*]. That may sound strange, but remember, God who created the entire universe by His spoken word tells us that a mystery "which from the beginning of the world hath been hid in God, who created all things by Jesus Christ: To the intent that now unto the principalities and powers in the heavenlies might be known by the church the manifold wisdom of God, According to the eternal purpose which he purposed in Christ Jesus *our Lord*" (Ephesians 3:9–11).

Notice that Almighty God the Father, by seating His Son on the throne at His right hand gave to His Son the authority to be *His* Lord. Then we are told that the intent or purpose in so doing was to make His Son *our* Lord! How could it be possible for Jesus Christ to be the Lord of lords and yet not be our Lord?

Now think about it. If God has yielded His Lordship to His Son, making Him the Lord of Lords, then it stands to reason that if we are to be called the children of God, we too must yield ourselves to the same Lordship. How can it be otherwise?

In Colossians 1:16–19, we read this amazing pronouncement: "For by him were all things created, that are in heaven, and that are in earth, visible and invisible, whether thrones, or dominions, or principalities, or powers: all things were created by him, and for him; And he is before all things, and by him all things consist. And he is the head [Lord] of the body, the church: who is the beginning, the firstborn from the dead; that in all things he might have the preeminence. For it pleased the Father that in him [Jesus] should all fulness dwell."

This passage tells us that Jesus Christ created everything, including you and me, by and for Himself, and that he is the Head [Lord] of the Church. Since He is the Head or Lord of the Church, He is the Lord over everyone who is a part of the Church. You cannot be in the body of Christ unless you worship Him as your Lord!

Romans 10:9–10 necessarily follows: "That if thou shalt *confess with thy mouth Jesus as Lord*, and shalt believe in thine heart that God hath raised him from the dead, thou shalt be saved. For with the heart man believeth unto righteousness; and with the mouth confession is made unto salvation." The Scripture declares emphatically that one must confess Christ as his or her Lord without hesitation—that is, with the mouth—in order to be saved. Paul repeats this truth in verse 13: "For whosoever will call upon the name of *the Lord* shall be saved." He doesn't say, the name of the Savior, but the name of the Lord! Clearly, to deny this truth is to deny that the Bible is the Word of God. It renders such a naysayer as an unregenerate sinner. To reject Jesus Christ as Lord is to refuse the salvation that He offers.

That's why the Lord Jesus said in Matthew 10:32–33, "Whosoever therefore shall confess me before men, him will I confess also before my Father which is in heaven. But whosoever shall deny me before men, him will I also deny before my Father which is in heaven." To confess Jesus Christ before men means that you must confess Him with your mouth: "That if thou shalt confess with thy mouth Jesus as Lord . . . ."

Such a verbal confession shows that you are not *ashamed* to be known as one who belongs to Jesus Christ as your Lord. Hence, Christ warns, "For whosoever shall be ashamed of me and of my words, of him shall the Son of man be ashamed, when he shall come in his own glory, and in his Father's, and of the holy angels" (Luke 9:26).

I wonder how anyone can debate or deny what God's Word declares. In Philippians 2:9–11, we read, "Wherefore God also hath *highly exalted* him [Christ], and given him *a name which is above every name*: That at the name of Jesus *every* knee should bow, of those in heaven, and those in earth, and those under the earth; And that *every* tongue should *confess that Jesus Christ is Lord*, to the glory of God the Father." Anyone who denies this most basic truth of God's Word is guilty of calling Almighty God a liar! That is the very person that Christ said He will deny before His Father and the angels in Heaven. That person will spend eternity in the Lake of Fire.

Every time the Lord Jesus Christ is so named, His name means three things. He is Lord (the *Supreme Authority and Master*), He is Jesus (*the Savior*), and He is Christ (*the Anointed One—the Messiah*). His name tells us that He is *anointed* by the Father to be our *Lord* and *Savior*. All three designations are required to provide us with eternal life.

Consider these things. Lucifer rebelled against God when he fought to claim his superiority over the Son of God; Adam and Eve rebelled against God by rejecting the Lordship of Christ and attempting to declare themselves to be His equal; the Jews rebelled against the authority of their eternal King by having Him crucified, claiming to be superior to Him; and all mankind has rebelled against the authority of Christ, declaring their independence or freedom to live in sin—thereby making themselves slaves to sin and death and the enemies of Christ. The only way anyone can restore himself is to turn from his sinful rebellion and confess Christ as the Lord of his life. This is the *only* means of salvation recorded in the New Testament.

As a reminder, the work of merely accepting Jesus as one's Savior is *never* mentioned in the Bible. It is pure fiction! But it is fiction that can easily lead a person to think that because he has "accepted" Christ as his Savior he has the so-called "freedom" to continue in sin. There is no freedom in sin. Sin enslaves and condemns the sinner to hell.

There are those who argue that everything that smacks of works, or speaks of faith or righteousness, always refers to the work of Christ in us—that we have nothing whatsoever to do with it. They say it is the Holy Spirit working through us. In other words, we *can't* do anything to serve the Lord. He does it all. Let me tell you that is sheer nonsense and makes God a liar!

Peter said in 1 Peter 1:21, in reference to faith and hope "that *your* faith and hope might be in God." Notice that he did not say that Christ's faith and hope in us might be in God.

James 2:17 tells us, "Even so faith, if it hath not works, is dead, being alone." Is it possible for Christ to have a dead faith? James goes on to say, "Yea, a man may say, thou hast faith, and I have works: shew me thy faith without works, and I will shew you *my* faith by *my* works." Did James take credit for what Jesus did for him? Certainly not. The Holy Spirit enables us to express our faith by our works, but that requires our willingness to obey Him.

Then in 4:17, James said, "Therefore to him that knoweth to do good, and doeth it not, to him it is sin." The implication according to the nay-sayers is that the failure of Christ to do good through a believer makes the believer a sinner! Now really! I am sure that Christ has never failed at anything.

Paul wrote to the Thessalonians, "We give thanks to God always for you all, making mention of you in our prayers; Remembering without ceasing *your work of faith*, and *labour of love*, and *patience of hope* in our Lord Jesus Christ, in the sight of God our Father" (1 Thessalonians 1:2–3). Once again we see Paul's recognition of the personal faith, love, and hope of those believers.

51

I could provide scores of references to the faith that is expressed by believers. The Greek word *pistis* translated "faith" means *persuasion. Pistis* is a derivative of the word *peitho* as in 2 Timothy 1:12 where Paul tells us, "I know whom I have believed, and am *persuaded* that he is able to keep that which I have committed unto him against that day." Faith or persuasion is not needed by our Lord, but is absolutely essential to the individual believer.

Ephesians 2:8–9 is a reminder to every born-again believer. When God says, "By grace are ye saved through faith," He is assuring us that we can accept His graciousness toward us as true—in this case, His graciousness in providing us with our salvation as the result of His gift [or *sacrificial offering* of Himself] because we believe Him when He says that He accomplished it on our behalf. Let me make it clear. The Greek does not say that our salvation is a gift as the result of our faith, but is, rather, the result of His sacrifice of Himself. *That* was *His* work, not ours. Therefore, no one can boast that the sacrifice was by his own effort. It was Christ's sacrifice of love and not ours. We don't have the bragging rights to any sacrificial work to obtain our salvation. The *sacrificing* was His work alone!

However, ask yourself: Is repentance a work of righteousness? Is confession a work of righteousness? Is commitment a work of righteousness? Is believing a work of righteousness? The answer to all of those questions is a resounding, "No!" No, because they are all required for salvation. It is by *His grace* through *our faith* that we are saved, but our faith includes all of these requirements. His grace is the gift of the sacrifice of His Son according to John 3:16.

The Lordship of Christ:

Romans 14:7–9 tells us, "For none of us liveth unto himself, and no man dieth unto himself. For whether we live, we live unto the Lord; and whether we die, we die unto the Lord: whether we live therefore, or die, we are the Lord's. *For to this end Christ both died, and rose, and revived, that he might be Lord both of the dead and living.*"

1. Question: According to Romans 14:7–9, why did Christ die, rise, and revive?

Romans 10:8–10 states that, "The word is nigh thee, even in thy mouth, and in thy heart; that is, the word of faith which we preach; That if thou shalt *confess Jesus as Lord* [the correct Greek text], and shalt believe in thine heart that God hath raised him from the dead, thou shalt be saved. For with the heart man believeth unto righteousness; and *with the mouth confession is made unto salvation.*" 10:13, "For whosoever shall *call upon the name of the Lord* shall be saved."

2. Question: According to Romans 10:8–10 & 13, what must you do to be saved?

Philippians 2:8–11, "And being found in fashion as a man, he humbled himself, and became obedient unto death, even the death of the cross. Wherefore God also hath highly exalted him, and given him a name which is above every name: That at the name of Jesus every knee should bow, of things in heaven, and things in earth, and things under the earth; And *that every tongue should confess that Jesus Christ is Lord, to the glory of God the Father.*"

3. Question: According to Philippians 2:8–10, how do we bring glory to God the Father?

Acts 2:34–36, "The Lord said unto my Lord, Sit thou on my right hand, until I make thy foes thy footstool. Therefore let all the house of Israel know assuredly, that God hath made that same Jesus, whom ye have crucified, both *Lord and Christ.*"

4. Question: According to Acts 2:34–36, who made Jesus both Lord and Christ?

John 13:13 (after Jesus had washed His disciples' feet), "Ye call me *Master and Lord*: and ye say well; *for so I am.*" In verse 16, Jesus went on to say, "Verily, verily I say unto you, *The servant is not greater than his Lord;* neither is he that is sent greater than he that sent him."

5. Question: According to John 13:13, who does Jesus say He is?

1 Corinthians 8:6, "But to us there is but one God, the Father, of whom are all things, and we in him; and one *Lord Jesus Christ, by whom are all things, and we by him.*"

6. Question: According to the above verse, what gives Jesus Christ the authority to declare Himself to be our Lord?

Hebrews 12:28–29,"Wherefore we *receiving a kingdom* which cannot be moved, let us have grace, whereby we may *serve God* acceptably with reverence and godly fear: For our God is a consuming fire."

8. Question: In return for the promise of our inheriting a kingdom, what is our present responsibility?

Colossians 3:23–24, "And whatsoever ye do, do it heartily, as to the Lord, and not unto men; Knowing that of the Lord *ye shall receive the reward of the inheritance: for ye serve the Lord Christ.*"

8. Question: How will our eternal reward be fulfilled in Heaven?

When asked by the rich young ruler in Mark 10:17–21, "Good Master, what shall I do that I may *inherit eternal Life?*" Jesus answered, "One thing thou lackest: go thy way, sell whatsoever thou hast, and give to the poor, and thou shalt have *treasure in heaven*: and come, *take up the cross, and follow me.* "

9. Question: How do we inherit eternal life?

Jesus said in John 12:26, "*If any man serve me,* let him follow me; and where I am, there shall also my servant be: if any man serve me, *him will my Father honour.*"

10. Question: What must we do in this life to receive honor from the Father?

In Revelation 7:15–17, regarding the redeemed after the day of redemption, we are told, "They are before the throne of God, and *serve him day and night* in his temple: and he that sitteth on the throne shall dwell among them. They shall hunger no more, neither thirst any more; neither shall the sun light on them, nor any heat. For the Lamb which is in the midst of the throne shall feed them, and shall lead them unto living fountains of waters: and God shall wipe away all tears from their eyes."

11. What will be our primary responsibility before the throne of God?

In Matthew 10:38, Jesus said, "*And he that taketh not his cross, and followeth after me, is not worthy of me.*"

12. Question: How are we made worthy of Christ?

Hebrews 12:14, "*Follow* peace with all men, and *holiness, without which no man shall see the Lord.*"

Jesus said in Matthew 5:8, "Blessed are the *pure in heart*: for they shall see God."

Romans 6:22, "But now being made free from sin, and become servants to God, ye have your fruit unto holiness, and the end everlasting life."

13. Question: What must we possess in order to see the Lord?

In 2 Timothy 4:10, Paul laments the fact that "Demas hath forsaken me, *having loved this present world.*"

14. Question: Why do people claim to be Christians and yet reject the Lord that bought them?

2 Timothy 2:19–21, "Nevertheless the foundation of God standeth sure, having this seal, The Lord knoweth them that are his. And, let every one that nameth the name of Christ *depart from iniquity.* But in a great house there are not only vessels of gold and silver, but also of wood and earth; and some to honour, and some to dishonour. If a man therefore purge himself from these, *he shall be a vessel unto honour, sanctified, and meet for the Master's use, and prepared unto every good work.*"

Jesus said in John 10:27–28, "My sheep hear my voice, and I know them, and *they follow me*: And I give unto them eternal life; and they shall never perish, neither shall any pluck them out of my hand."

1 John 2:4, "*He that saith, I know him, and keepeth not his commandments, is a liar, and the truth is not in him.*"

3 John 1, "Beloved, follow not that which is evil, but that which is good. *He that doeth good is of God*: but he that doeth evil hath not seen God."

15. How does the Lord know them that are His?

Jude 4, "For there are certain men crept in unawares, who were before of old *ordained to this condemnation*, ungodly men, turning the grace of our God into lasciviousness, and *denying the only Lord God, and our Lord Jesus Christ*."

Matthew 10:32–33, "Whosoever therefore shall confess me before men, him will I also confess before my Father which is in heaven. But *whosoever shall deny me before men, him will I also deny before my Father which is in heaven*."

16. Question: What happens to those who deny the Lord Jesus Christ?

Remember this: the reason God saves us by His grace is so that we are enabled to do good works! Ephesians 2:8–10 explains it this way: "For *by grace are ye saved* through faith; and that not of yourselves: it is the gift of God: Not of works, lest any man should boast. For *we are his workmanship, created in Christ Jesus unto good works*, which God hath before ordained [Greek: *prepared for us before we were saved*] that we should walk in them."

17. Question: What is included in <u>the gift of God</u>?

About the Author

Larry D. Rudder is a graduate of Southern Illinois University at Edwardsville, Illinois with a B.A. in History and Government, and an M.S. ED and S.D. in Counselor Education. He is also a graduate of Moody Bible Institute and studied Bible at Wheaton College.

He began preaching at the age of 18 and has conducted revival and evangelistic meetings across the country for over fifty years. He has written a number of gospel songs and recorded them with his wife Jeanette, while Dove award winner Henry Slaughter produced and played the keyboards for the recordings.

He is the author of *Christ at the Dinner Table, Christ in All His Glory, The Way of the Cross,* and two focus books: *The Great Confession* and *Selling Jesus.*